GALAPAGOS ISLANDS

A Traveler's Preview

by Kit and Art Lane

Pavilion Press
P.O. Box 250
Douglas, Mi 49406

Copyright 1989
By Pavilion Press

All rights reserved.

ISBN 1-877703-13-3

LC # 89-062878

GALAPAGOS ISLANDS

A Traveler's Preview

- Darwin

- Wolf

PACIFIC OCEAN

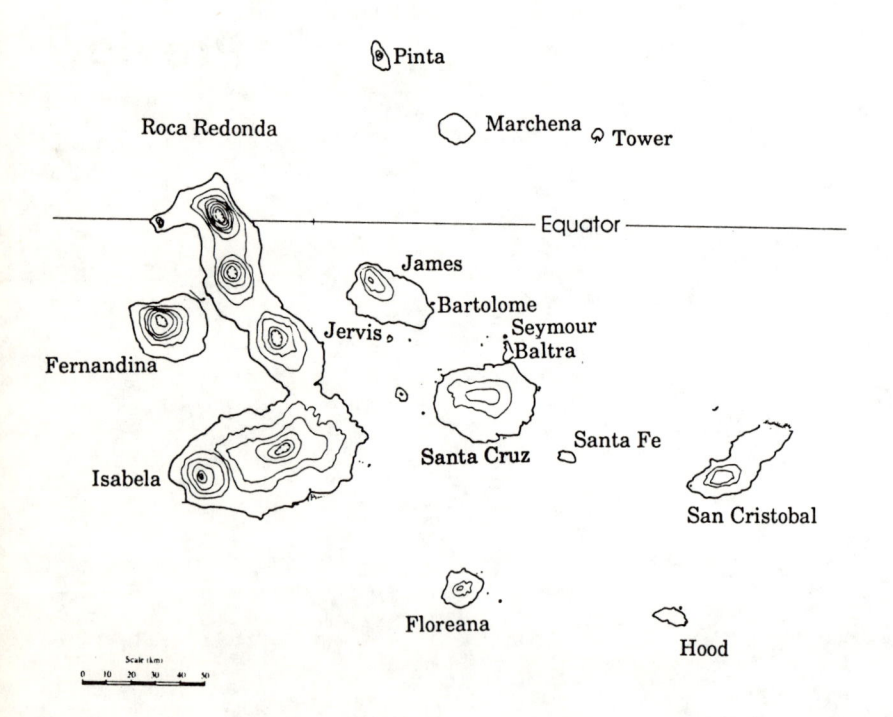

Pinta

Roca Redonda Marchena Tower

— Equator —

James
Bartolome
Jervis Seymour
Baltra
Fernandina

Isabela Santa Cruz Santa Fe

San Cristobal

Floreana Hood

Scale (km)
0 10 20 30 40 50

Table of Contents

1. The Enchanted Islands 5
2. History and Background 7
3. When to Go and How 10
4. Choosing Your Boat 13
5. Island Etiquette 16
6. Island by Island 24
7. Miscellaneous 48

*The Enchanted Isles
are like a zoo,
each venue separated
by water from the next,
each dot of land
differing from its neighbor
in subtle ways
only the creatures
that live there
truly understand.*

The Enchanted Islands

Early navigators and explorers called the archipelago of islands we know today as the Galapagos "La Encantadas Islas", the Enchanted (or Bewitched) Islands. Everything about them was strange, their birds, their tortoises, the lack of mammals, the climate, the currents and winds, and old deckhands would tell you the islands had a weird way of moving about the sea in a fog.

The enchantment remains today. A visit to the Galapagos Islands is "just a little bit off the ground," to use a Hollywood expression meaning that there is a suspension of reality, of the rules of nature as we know them. You are sure of it the first time you step up to the booby colonies and two thousand birds pretend you are not there at all. Snorkelers notice it when they see the fuzzy little muzzle of a curious sea lion poking into their masks, and a brown pelican plunges into the water less than ten feet away in pursuit of a fish. When a tropic bird with his two-foot tail streaming out behind circles your boat, peering in the dining room windows you know this is someplace special.

The air of enchantment is heightened by the logistics of a visit. Except for the four inhabited islands visitors must be back on their boats by sundown. Most nights the boats then anchor in a protected cove until after dinner. As their passengers bed down for the night, the captain starts the engines and steers through the darkness for another island. The travelers awake in the morning, usually already anchored in the quiet cove of a new adventure.

History and Background

The Galapagos Islands are of volcanic origin and are thought to be at least three million years old. They appear to lie over a "hot spot" which periodically pushes new volcanoes up from the earth's crust. Their massive undersea structures lie on the Nazca Plate, which is slowly drifting toward South America. Thus, the islands toward the east appear to have been formed first; they are more eroded and have more vegetation. The islands toward the west are newer, have less vegetation, and are still being enlarged by lava flows from time to time. Although most of the islands bear the cones of thousands of eruptions, large and small, four or five appear to have been formed by upheavals from the bottom of the sea. Their lava flows are layered with strata of limestone containing marine fossils. The island group lies about 600 miles west of South America and does not appear to have had a connection to the mainland.

The islands were discovered in 1525 by Tomas de Berlanga, the Bishop of Panama, when his becalmed ship was carried by an ocean current westward from Ecuador. For many years pirates and renegades used the islands as a haven. English buccaneers utilized them as a base to

GALAPAGOS ISLANDS

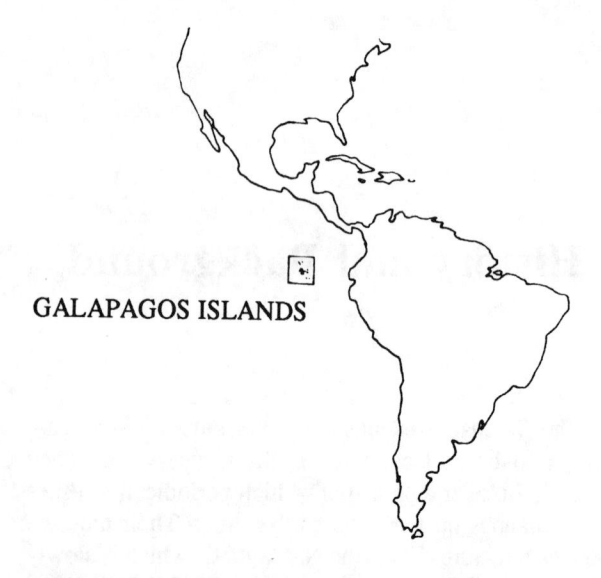

attack Spanish ships and towns along the coast of South America. Whaling vessels called there. Ships of many nations captured the abundant, slow-moving tortoises and stored them in holds where they provided food for months at sea. The government of Ecuador claimed the islands in 1832. Settlement started then, and the pioneers brought with them animals such as cattle, pigs, dogs, cats, rats and mice which, on some islands, severely damaged the native plants and animals.

The islands' most famous visitor was Charles Darwin, who studied the flora and fauna for several weeks in 1835 during the five-year round-the-world trip of the British survey ship *HMS Beagle*. The variations in tortoises from island to island and the different species of finches found on most islands helped get Darwin thinking about natural selection, which resulted, 25 years later, in his book, *Origin of Species*.

In 1959, recognizing the need to preserve the islands in as natural a state as possible, Ecuador designated all the uninhabited areas of the islands as the nation's first national park. At the same time the Charles Darwin Foundation for the Galapagos Islands set up the Charles Darwin Research Station on Santa Cruz. The station assists the national park staff in its work. The goals of the research station are to support scientific investigation, advise the park administration, help establish conservation programs, and appeal internationally for conservation funds.

Despite more than 150 years of settlement, the Galapagos Islands have only a few small towns and only four of the islands are inhabited. Most of the land is in the national park. There aren't many jobs, yet the Galapagos Islands are seen as sort of a frontier by mainland Ecuadorians looking for a new start. Each year some Ecuadorians make the trip to the islands looking for a greener pasture which, for most, isn't there. But for the wildlife, things are looking up. The government is working to eradicate introduced animals, has a limit on the number of tourists who can visit the islands, and so far has resisted the temptation to build hotels on solitary isles where now there is only lava, cactus and wildlife.

When to Go and How

VISA: The Galapagos Islands, or more properly the Archipelago de Colon although they are seldom called by their correct name except in the most official of government documents, are a province of Ecuador. North American travelers need only a passport, valid for the length of their stay, to enter Ecuador. A visitor's visa, valid for up to 90 days, is issued at the border. More than 90 percent of the archipelago is a National Park and there is a $40 per person fee (payable in U. S. currency) to enter

The National Park visa stamp features a Galapagos tortoise.

the National Park. This fee is collected at the airport when you land on the islands, and a special "visa" to enter the National Park will be issued.

GETTING THERE: The mainland Ecuadorian city of Guayaquil is the jumping-off place for a visit to the islands. Even visitors who go to Quito first must fly to Guayaquil before crossing the 600 miles of Pacific Ocean between the continent of South America and the Galapagos Islands. The airlines recommend that travelers arrive at the airport two and a half hours before the flight. There are times, in the confusion of the Guayaquil airport that this is not a moment too soon. Although there is no regular passenger boat service between the Galapagos and the mainland, freighters and cruise boats, outbound after repairs, will sometimes carry passengers. The service is erratic at best, and advance reservations for a specific departure day are even less likely.

SIDETRIPS: In addition to the enchanted Galapagos Islands, the country of Ecuador has mountains and rain forests, Indian villages and modern cities and is well worth a stay of several days or weeks. The most popular excursion combined with a trip to the Galapagos is an exploration of another ecosystem that is a novelty to North Americans, the Amazon jungle. In a region known as El Oriente, the Amazon River begins its trek through the heart of South America to the Atlantic Ocean. Tours can be booked from Quito and may include a trip in a dugout canoe and overnight stays in floating hotels on the river itself. The highlands north of Quito are another popular sidetrip. Here the draw is spectacular mountain scenery and colorful Indian markets where baskets, inexpensive knitted goods, leather items, and wood carvings may be purchased. Each little community seems to specialize in a particular craft.

CLIMATE: Although the islands sit squarely on the equator, the expected hot climate is mitigated by cold waters carried from the Antarctic by the Humboldt Current. January to April are usually the warmest months, July to November the coolest times. Rainfall can be very erratic, with recorded annual accumulations of as little as one inch or as much as 55 inches on the coast. Inland the recorded extremes are 15 and 80 inches. The major factor in this wide variation is in the currents. Some years a south-flowing current, called El Nino, overpowers the cold waters being brought northward by the Humboldt current, and warmer waters surround the islands. El Nino years are frequently associated with very hot weather. Rarely, the condition may persist for more than a year before the colder currents push in again and the area returns to its normal climatic cycle. Most hotels and boats are air conditioned or otherwise equipped to make even less-than-ideal weather tolerable to the tourist.

ARRIVAL: Planes from Guayaquil land at the island of Baltra using a portion of an airport built by U. S. forces during World War II. There is a shuttle bus that links the new open-air terminal building with the old military docks on the southwestern shore, where boats, both large and small, are boarded for island tours. There is also a ferry boat which takes passengers from Baltra to the northern coast of Santa Cruz, meeting there a bus which traverses the island north to south, ending in Puerto Ayora on Academy Bay. In the late 1980s regular plane service was begun from the Ecuadorian mainland to San Cristobal. A bus carries passengers from the airport to the docks at Puerto Baquerizo Moreno, the oldest of the fishing villages, which serves as home port for the 90-passenger *MV Galapagos Explorer*. There is also a ferry boat operated by INGALA which links Santa Cruz and San Cristobal twice a week and provides every other week service to the settlements on Isabela.

Choosing Your Boat

The typical tourist in the Galapagos does not stay in a hotel (although there are a few small ones on two of the islands, and guest house arrangements can be made in other places), eat in a restaurant, or visit a bar ashore. The average time spent in the shops is about two hours. Eating, sleeping, and spare time between island visits is spent aboard a boat. The Galapagos cruise boats fall into three general categories.

LARGE CRUISE SHIPS: The largest ship allowed to tour in the islands has passenger accommodations for 90. This number is the largest group that can be allowed at any one time on most of the islands. These ships are the *MV Santa Cruz* and the *MV Bucanero*, operating out of Baltra, and the *MV Galapagos Explorer* which began operations in 1989 using San Cristobal as home port. Typically these boats carry a band for dance and dinner music, bars that serve liquid refreshment (and sometimes snacks) all day long, and have air conditioned cabins with private bath and showers. Some offer extra amenities like swimming pools, boutiques, a library, and other social activities. There may be as many as five or six naturalist guides aboard who offer evening educational sessions and

Riding the panga ashore with a guide on the bow.

accompany the passengers in groups of no more than 20 on shore excursions. The larger boats specialize in three to five day cruises.

TOUR BOATS: Smaller than the cruise boats, the regular tour boats usually serve eight to 34 passengers and may be booked entirely by one tour company, or may include passengers from a number of different tours. A naturalist guide is required for every 20 passengers, but many boats carry extra guides to accommodate passengers who speak different languages. Some of these boats are quite new and luxurious with private facilities for each cabin and sumptuous buffet dinners. Some are far more basic with shared facilities and dinners which emphasize the fishing skills of the crew and captain. Most boats have some provision for beverage service, both alcoholic and non-alcoholic. Often drinks are kept in an accessible cooler. Passengers keep a running tab that is settled up the last day of the voyage. Cruises of from three to ten days are common.

YACHTS: Tour boats (described above) are nautically classed as yachts but are usually booked by a tour company and space sold to the passengers. The yachts-for-hire that work in the Galapagos tour trade are usually booked by (or for) individual passengers. They house two to twelve visitors and vary their touring program in accordance with the wishes of those who hire them. Some of these boats are sailboats, or have sailing capabilities, although the winds of the Galapagos do not offer ideal sailing conditions. They carry a minimum staff of four, the captain, cook, cabin boy, and a naturalist guide, each assisting the others as needed. It is possible to sail your own, or a rented private yacht, to the islands, but you are not permitted to navigate among the islands or land in the National Park. Those with their own boats must anchor in Academy Bay or Wreck Bay and use a Galapagos ship with a certified guide to tour the islands.

DAY TRIPS: For those with a very limited amount of time short trips to islands near Baltra can be arranged that give at least a small taste of the wonders of the islands. Overnight accommodations are available on Santa Cruz.

Island Etiquette

In 1959 all areas of the Galapagos Islands, except those already colonized by that date, were declared a National Park. In 1979 the islands were declared a World Heritage Site by the member states of UNESCO (United Nations Educational, Scientific, and Cultural Organization, an arm of the United Nations). This designation marks the Galapagos as one of the world's most significant natural areas, and highlights the need for conservation as "a unique part of mankind's natural heritage."

To minimize the impact of tourism on the fragile ecology of the islands the National Park office has set an annual quota of tourists, as well as a daily quota for most of the islands, and decreed that no one should set foot ashore except when accompanied by a naturalist guide, trained and approved at the Darwin Research Station on Santa Cruz. Each guide must have an itinerary approved by the National Park office to avoid too many visitors on any one island and must limit the size of escorted groups to 20.

A tourist pauses to put on her shoes after a wet landing on Santa Fe, a few feet from a mother sea lion nursing her pup.

LANDINGS: Because nearly all of the boats used for inter-island travel have too deep a draft to land on the islands, tourists are conveyed from their boats to the landing sites by motorized dinghies, known locally as pangas. Each island that is open to tourists has one or more approved landing areas. According to facilities provided these landings are spoken of as "wet" or "dry" landings. A dry landing is one where there is a jetty or rock that under most circumstances you should be able to step onto without getting your feet wet. Some of the stone jetties are in poor repair and some may not be available at all tide levels, but your guide should warn you ahead of time if there is a serious chance that you might get wet feet. In general the dress for a dry landing is shoes and socks since most Galapagos rock is some form of lava and difficult to walk on barefooted. A wet landing is one where there is no dock and the visitor can expect to get wet, occasionally to the waist. Most wet landings occur on open beaches when the operator runs the panga up on the sand on an incoming wave. As the water ebbs, as many passengers as possible swing over the side and scramble up the beach before the next wave arrives. Although canvas footwear is recommended for all landings, most wet landings on sand beaches can be accomplished safely with bare feet. Shoes, cameras and other needed items should be carried ashore in waterproof bags.

TRAILS: Most of the visitor sites will have trails designated by wooden stakes pounded in the ground or in cracks in the rocks. Although the route you must take is designated, usually no attempt has been made to clear a path or provide secure footing. Many of the rocks on which you step will be unstable, and there are many places where the path will require jumping from one rock to the next. Test each step and do not try to rush. Birds and animals that nest on the path (because it is less cluttered) are an added hazard. It is permissible to leave the path to avoid a nest or a protective mama booby, but the deviation should be as brief as possible. If your way is blocked by a sea lion or seal, do not step over the animal as if he were a sleeping pet on your floor at home. You may miss and step on him, or he might wake up suddenly and not understand what is happening. Both sea lions and iguanas will usually move away if you clap your hands together rapidly while walking slowly toward them.

ANIMAL CONTACT: The official rules decree that "Animals may not be touched or handled. All wild animals dislike this and will quickly lose their remarkable tameness if thus treated by human invaders." There are times that avoiding contact takes concentration. Because the animals and birds do not scurry away at your approach, the primary concern is that you might accidentally step on one. Watch especially for gray marine iguanas that like to sleep in cracks of similar colored rocks with their tails hanging out. Sea lions during the heat of the day will snooze under a bush. Visitors walking around the bush might discover that their feet are inches from an animal's nose. Yellow warblers will play around your feet until you fear you may step on one. Sea lions, some birds, and iguanas will advance toward the visitor with curiosity, but they will back off warily if you begin advancing toward them. In the water, sea lions will swim around you, even through your legs, but they will probably not make contact. In general the wildlife will simply act as though you are not there at all. There are a couple of exceptions. When making a landing it is a good idea to scan the area for a bull sea lion, and stay as far from him as is practical. He may decide you are an competitor and try to drive you off, or that you are a desirable female that he wants to add to his harem. Either situation could be difficult. If he advances toward you (and they can move with remarkable agility) back off quickly. He will generally not continue in pursuit if you retreat. If he keeps up his nervous behavior, it may be a good idea to stay away from his wives and children as well. The second most troublesome encounter can be with a parent booby on the trail defending a nest or a chick, especially if there is no easy alternate route. If you get really close, usually less than a foot, the parent bird will clack its bill and threaten. In rare instances a booby may peck at your leg as you go by. It might be a good idea to put your camera bag or extra shirt between your leg and the angry bird. Mockingbirds, especially the aggressive species on Hood, may jump on you as you sunbathe on the beach. Just shoo them away.

NESTING COLONIES: On the nest, or with young, birds are at their most skittish. When you visit areas where nesting activity is going on, be especially careful to move smoothly and quietly to avoid startling parent birds from the nest. Often when they leave in a flurry they knock the egg or chick to the ground. Their absence leavesthe young one or egg exposed to the sun, a condition that can be fatal in less than 20 minutes. Frigate birds, hawks and other predators also threaten unguarded chicks.

FOOD: No food of any kind is to be taken to the uninhabited islands. This is to avoid introducing food insects, seeds, or other organisms that might upset the islands' ecosystems. Food is not to be offered to any bird or animal to avoid the spread of unwanted seeds and because feeding can destroy the social structure. The aim in the Galapagos is to let plants and animals continue in as close to a natural situation as possible. Because of the heat of the sun you are permitted to take a thermos or bottle of water, but it is to be drunk as carefully as possible to avoid spilling the water (and possible foreign organisms) onto the ground. There are no toilets on the uninhabited islands, and visitors are asked to use only shipboard facilities.

PETS: Do not bring pets of any kind to the Galapagos Islands. Some of the most destructive forces in the archipelago are domesticated animals brought in by man that have reverted to a wild state. Horses, cattle, burros, dogs, pigs, cats, and especially goats have seriously damaged the ecology of several islands. In some cases the National Park Service is working on their extermination.

TAKE ONLY PICTURES: No plant, animal or remains of them (shells, bones, pieces of wood, feathers, etc.) are to be removed from the islands, or disturbed. This extends to underwater organisms (dead or alive). For this reason the Park Service asks that you not buy any souvenirs made from plants or animals of the islands, for example, coral or shell jewelry, or items made of tortoise shell. They ask that you be especially careful not to transport live material to the islands or from island to island. Make sure that there are no seeds or insects in your cuffs, pockets, or on the bottom of your shoes. When you leave an island and before boarding your boat, a crew member usually hoses down your bare feet and legs. The panga driver may ask you to wash off the soles of your shoes to avoid bringing sand or mud onboard the boat. This is not just a housekeeping problem but is designed to avoid introducing seeds or spores to another island. Each land body in the Galapagos has its own fauna and flora, and introduced plants and animals can quickly destroy this uniqueness.

LITTER: Be especially careful of litter (film boxes, wrappers, etc.). Most boats encourage each passenger to carry a litter bag not only to transport his own litter back to the boat but also to help keep the islands clean. Smoking on the islands is discouraged following some serious fires on Isabela in the late 1970s. If visitors do smoke on the beaches, they are asked to take all matches and cigarette butts back to the boats for proper disposal. Trash thrown overboard or left on land can cause serious, even fatal, injury to animals and birds.

SWIMMING: You will probably have many opportunities to swim during your visit. Your guide will show you the safe areas and make suggestions. There are some hazards to swimming in the waters surrounding the Galapagos Islands. The most common problem is an encounter with the spines of the sea urchin. The sting can be quite painful, although an old island remedy, the application of human urine, is said to work as well as anything to relieve the pain. When you get back to the boat, look carefully to make sure that there is not a small piece of the spine remaining under the skin. You will notice sharks and both manta and stingrays in the waters, but they are not aggressive toward humans. One guide claimed that a favorite sport is to slip up behind a white-tipped shark and tug on his tail. This is not necessarily a good idea, but it is indicative of the placid nature of the marine life in Galapagos waters. The use of a snorkel and mask is recommended to allow easier observation of the underwater plant and animal life. When they see visitors splashing around, sea lions usually come over to play and will swim in circles around you, dive between your legs, or paddle in front with their heads dipped backwards (because their eyes are designed to see better underwater). One old-fashioned Galapagos sport is to ride the giant sea turtles as they swim ashore to lay their eggs. This is not a good idea. Not only does it violate the rules against touching the animals, but it also ignores the fact that the female turtles after the arduous task of mating and egg laying are usually very tired.

TURTLE NESTS: During the season that sea turtles come ashore to lay their eggs, the sands of the beach may look like the site of a tank war. At the end of the tank-tread looking track of the female turtle there is usually a depression in the sand which may be as large as five feet in diameter. This is the nest site. Do not walk on these areas to avoid damage to the freshly laid eggs.

DAILY ROUTINE: Although the days in the islands vary, a generalized routine would be breakfast at 7:30 or 8 a.m., followed by a short break and the boarding of the panga for a trip ashore. The trip ashore will probably last two to three hours, and there may be opportunity for swimming before returning to the boat about 11:30 a.m. There is usually a brief time until lunch is served about noon. After lunch, if a change in venue is planned, the boat may make a short journey to another visitor site or another island. Visitors are taken ashore in the panga for another two to three-hour visit to points of interest. This visit is usually followed by a swim on the beach, or sometimes a panga visit to an interesting snorkel site, or a swim off the fantail of the boat. When the tourists return from this trip about 5:30 or just before 6 p.m. (when the sun sets and all must be off the island), they are usually offered some snack to tide them over until dinner. Dinner is usually served about 7:30 p.m. After dinner the visitors chat, read and write while the crew washes dishes in the galley. When chores are done, the captain raises anchor and heads for the next island, arriving at the next destination some time in the night, midnight to near dawn depending on distance.

Island by Island

A multiplicity of names is a Galapagos tradition. Although the islands had received the title "Insulae de los Galopegos" (Islands of the Tortoises) as early as 1570, they were also called La Encantadas (The Enchanted or Bewitched). When they were officially annexed to Ecuador in 1832, they were named "Archipelago del Ecuador." In 1892 in honor of the 400th anniversary of the discovery of the Americas by Christopher Columbus they received their present official name "Archipelago de Colon." They are far more commonly called the Galapagos Islands, or simply "The Galapagos."

In similar fashion each of the major islands and many of the smaller ones have more than one name. Most have at least two, one English and one Spanish, and several have additional choices. When the Columbian anniversary was being celebrated in 1892, the government officially changed the English names using many names associated with Columbus and his voyages, including that of his boats (*Santa Maria* and *Pinta*), the names of the King and Queen of Spain who supported him financially (Isabela and Fernandina) and their country (Espanola), the traditional birthplace of Columbus (Genovesa), his patron saint (San Cristobal) and the first landfall of Columbus in the new world (San Salvador). In present day practice most inhabited islands are given their Spanish names, while the uninhabited ones are more likely to retain the English appellation, but there is no unanimity of opinion on this. In the island by island survey below an attempt is made to list all of the names the visitor is likely to encounter.

Baltra

Also known as South Seymour, Baltra is located north of the large island of Santa Cruz. Until the improvement of the small air strip on San Cristobal in 1988, Baltra was the only landing place for planes from the mainland. A majority of air traffic still enters through Baltra where a new terminal building and customs house, built in the middle 1980s, replaced facilities left by the United States armed forces following World War II. The air base and docking facilities at Baltra were expected to play a major role in the defense of the Panama Canal if the Japanese front moved to the eastern Pacific, but the war never came to the Galapagos Islands. Prior to the establishment of the base iguanas were abundant on Baltra, but they were exterminated by troops stationed there both to avoid their presence on the runways and as an antidote for boredom. Many of the larger birds shared a similar fate, and today there is little life on Baltra except for an occasional finch or visiting gull, and a particularly prolific house mouse which is threatening the already scant vegetation. An asphalt road links the air field with the docks left behind at Aeolean Cove. A bus takes incoming passengers to the docks to meet their tour boats or the ferry to Santa Cruz.

Seymour

Originally called North Seymour, it is now officially Seymour. A tiny island north of Baltra it is host to a Magnificent Frigatebird colony, nesting Blue-footed Boobies, and it is the place a visitor is most likely to see a Short-eared Owl. The landing is dry but may be particularly difficult at certain tides or in a rough sea. On the edge of Seymour there is a colony of Galapagos Fur Seals, and, nearby on a small island called Mosquera, a colony of sea lions. The easiest way to tell a sea lion from a fur seal is to look at the face. The sea lion has a more pointed nose, finer features, and usually smoother fur. The fur seal has a face that more resembles a bear and is fuzzier all over. Marine iguanas nest on the rocks on the edges of Seymour. When most of the land iguanas were removed from Baltra during World War II, three specimens were transferred to Seymour including the single largest land iguana ever discovered on the islands which weighed in at over 16 pounds. They were later removed to the Darwin Research Station to participate in a captive breeding program.

Santa Cruz

Santa Cruz (Spanish for "Holy Cross") is the island cited when the name problems of the Galapagos are discussed because it has had no less than eight recorded names: Bolivia, Norfolk, Porter. Valdez, Chavez, San Clemente, Indefatigable and Santa Cruz. It is located near the geographical center of the archipelago and is the site of the national park headquarters and the Charles Darwin Research Station. Puerto Ayora, the largest town on the island is located on the southern shore at Academy Bay (named for the sailing schooner Academy which served a group of scientists from the California Academy of Sciences in the islands for 12 months in 1905-06).

Visitors take close-up pictures of giant tortoises at the Darwin Research Station on Santa Cruz.

Starting from a desert coastal plain the road across the terrain rises rapidly eventually reaching a height of 2,835 feet above sea level. The temperature drops. Humidity (and frequently mist or rainfall) increases. At the top of the island there is a series of pit craters, the result of the surface layers of lava subsiding around a fissure over a subsurface magma chamber, and bracken covers the sides of old volcanoes. The highlands of Santa Cruz provide habitat for some of the largest tortoises still found in the wild. A public bus runs on the paved road that bisects the island, ending at the north coast where a ferry boat conveys passengers to the dock at Baltra, and thence by bus to the airport. Although pirates and others had called at the island in earlier days, the first permanent settlement was by a group of Norwegians at Puerto Ayora in 1926. There are now two smaller villages located at higher elevation in the midst of prime farming land, Bellavista, directly north of Puerto Ayora, and Santa Rosa, closer to the center of the island, both on the bus route. The 3000-plus residents of Puerto Ayora are engaged in fishing, boat-building, and serving the research station and tourist trade. There are a number of tourist-geared stores with post cards, books, Ecuadorian souvenirs, unusual designer shirts and other clothing with a Galapagos theme. At least five small hotels provide overnight accommodation and a number of restaurants and nightclubs offer diversion to the tourists in port. Visiting tour boats and yachts anchor in the bay, with the larger boats just outside the bay, and tourists are conveyed to the downtown docks by panga. There is also a water taxi on the bay which will take you to your boat if you miss your panga driver. The inter-island ferry boat also must be boarded in mid-bay. Inquire about schedules and tickets at the INGALA office, across from the park near the town dock at the west edge of downtown. A short walk uphill from the public dock east of downtown near the national park headquarters brings visitors to the Charles Darwin Foundation Research Station. The facility is the outgrowth of a 1954-55 Submarine Research Expedition led by Hans Hass. Irenaus Eibl-Eibesfeldt, who was on the earlier expedition, was asked to make a survey in 1957 for UNESCO in cooperation with the International Council for Bird Preservation, the New York Zoological Society, Time,Inc., and the government of Ecuador to study the conservation problems and to choose a site for a research station. In 1959 on the centenary of the publication of Darwin's *Origin of Species* a research station was founded near the shores of Academy Bay and formally dedicated in

January of 1964. In addition to providing facilities for visiting scientists, and the operation of weather, seismographic and oceanographic stations, the research center has an on-going program of captive breeding for endangered tortoises and iguanas. It is also the home of Lonesome George, the last remaining specimen of the Pinta island tortoise. In 1973 the Van Straelen Museum (named for the first president of the Charles Darwin Foundation) opened. Technicians and researchers at the station are also involved with an on-going program to eradicate introduced animals from selected islands. Although efforts continue with other species and on other islands, goats have already been cleared from Hood, Plaza, Santa Fe, Jervis, and Marchena, and the battle with rats was declared won on Bartolome. The island of Santa Cruz has also been mentioned as a place where pirate ships headed with their gold and other loot, some becoming wrecked on the rocky shores, sending the gold to the bottom of the sea. In addition to the two docks at Academy Bay, there is a visitor site on the northern shore at Turtle Cove. It is a popular turtle nesting area, and its black rocks and shore usually contain an exceptionally large number of bright red Sally Lightfoot Crabs. A lagoon just over a sandy rise from the turtle nesting area is frequently inhabited by Greater Flamingos, White-cheeked Pintail Ducks, and shore birds. It is also one of the best places in the islands for Great Blue, Lava and Striated Herons. The landing at Turtle Cove is a wet landing on a sandy beach. Since it is a short distance from the boat landing at Baltra, it is often the first place visited. West of Academy Bay is a large sandy beach usually called Tortuga Beach. It is within walking distance of Puerto Ayora and is a popular place among the residents. It is one of the few beaches in the Galapagos where picnicking is permitted.

Plaza Islets

Located less than a mile east of Santa Cruz, North Plaza and South Plaza look like a pair of sideways parentheses. They are named for a former president of Ecuador. Because of their location so near Academy Bay and only a short distance from the landing at Baltra, a survey in 1980 indicated that more tourists visited South Plaza island than any other single island in the archipelago. South Plaza affords a dry landing, but an active colony of sea lions along that beach, means the visitors must be on the lookout for the dominant bull and often must shoo lounging animals from the jetty. It is a small island, a half mile long by about 150 yards wide, sloping from the southern beach to a cliff on the northern side that is 40 to 50 feet high. The dominant vegetation is vesuvium, an abundant colorful plant a few inches high, and opuntia cactus. The cacti support a large land iguana population. This is also an island with an unusually large number of Lava Lizards. On the rocky northern shore is a colony of bachelor sea lions that must climb the steep rock cliff on their return from the sea. Many bear recent injuries or scars of unsuccessful fights with the harem boss of the South Plaza colony. Also on the rocky cliff are nesting Shearwaters, Swallow-Tailed Gulls, and Red-Billed Tropicbirds. The protected area between the two Plazas is a favorite spot for snorkelers.

Santa Fe

Santa Fe (the English island of Barrington, named after Admiral Samuel Barrington) is located between Santa Cruz and San Cristobal. It has a harbor protected by lava outcroppings, with several interesting brain coral formations. A visit calls for a wet landing on a sloping yellow sand beach, usually well populated with sea lions. The flat part of the island has many large and well-developed cactus plants. A short walk leads to a steep escarpment with quite different vegetation. The population of land iguanas, both on the flats and in the highlands, has been increasing rapidly following the extermination of the feral goat population by 1985.

San Cristobal

The island of San Cristobal, formerly Chatham (named for William Pitt, the Earl of Chatham), is the easternmost island in the archipelago, and the capital of the Ecuadorian province of Galapagos. The village of Puerto Baqueurizo Moreno on Wreck Bay on the western tip contains the government offices and buildings, two or three small hotels, docks, and processing plants for the local fishing industry. Prior to 1988 San Cristobal was not a popular tourist stop. That year a small airstrip not far from the village was expanded to accommodate air traffic from the mainland and the *MV Galapagos Explorer*, one of the larger touring boats, began operation in 1989 using Puerto Baqueurizo Moreno as its home base. The island was visited by Darwin in 1835. It was an early base for pirates and, later, whaling ships. In the latter half of the seventeenth century Manuel Cobos founded a settlement above Wreck Bay called Progreso which was to be an agricultural settlement raising fresh fruit and vegetables for sale to the whaling ships. The laborers were mainly convicts and slaves originally from the mainland who had been sent to a penal colony on Floreana. They were cruelly treated by Cobos whose favorite punishments seemed to be lethal floggings and maroonings on uninhabited islands with no food or fresh water. Eventually the workers rose up in rebellion and killed him in bed. The population of the island also grew following a slave revolt on Floreana in the 1870s. The agricultural settlement, El Progreso, still exists east of the capital. The natural rock formation, known as Leon Dormido or

Kicker Rock, is a tourist draw on San Cristobal. The island is also the only place in the world to see the Chatham mockingbird, one of four species of mockingbirds that inhabit the Galapagos Islands.

Hood

Hood Island (named for Admiral Viscount Samuel Hood) is the southernmost Galapagos Island. Its Spanish name is Espanola (a variation of Espana, Spain). It is best known as one of the few nesting places in the world of the Waved Albatross. The colony is a short walk from the wet landing at Punta Suarez at the northeast tip. The birds begin to arrive in late March and prepare for nesting with a complicated display of bill clacking and dueling. May and June are nesting months, and the last of the young fledge in January. From then until the last of May the colony is deserted. Albatrosses can soar at sea for many months, sleeping and eating on the wing, but they have problems getting launched. Near their nesting grounds the U.S. Navy built a road during the war to service a radar installation. It is this road that many of the birds use as a take-off pad, patting the ground with their feet while simultaneously flailing about with their wings until they are airborne. The Hood island population is estimated at 12,000 pairs. There is also a large Blue-footed Booby colony, a smaller Masked Booby breeding ground, and an unusual subspecies of marine iguana which sports shades of aqua and red. Near the seabird colonies is a rock formation that forms a blowhole at certain tides, shooting water 30 to 70 feet in the air. A second popular visitor site on Hood is Gardner Bay, a white sand beach on the north coast facing the small island of Gardner-near-Hood. It is a wet landing. Swimming is excellent and usually includes a chance to cavort with the Hood Island sea lions. There is also a good chance that at least one pair of American Oystercatchers will be present along the beach.

Also very obvious on the beach at Gardner Bay is the Hood Mockingbird, the largest and most aggressive of the four species that are found in the Galapagos. The mockingbirds will trail after visitors in a threatening manner as they walk on the beach. They seldom make contact and will retreat when you advance toward them, but their persistence is sometimes unnerving. Sunbathers who lie still for a period of time will often get an inquisitive bird on their stomachs or backs, bent on an explorative foray. Hair ribbons, film wrappers, combs, pens, or any items small enough may be carried off by the marauding mockingbirds. The Hood Mockingbird is endemic and found only on Hood and Gardner-near-Hood.

Floreana

The official name of Floreana is Santa Maria (for Columbus's flagship), and its English name was Charles (for King Charles II), but it is always called Floreana. It is the island with the longest history of human settlement. There are a number of stories about its earliest inhabitants which have been told and retold, sometimes overlapping, sometimes conflicting. It was a favorite stop for pirates and whalers because of its fresh water springs and sheltering caves. The first permanent resident on Floreana, indeed in all the Galapagos was Patrick Watkins, originally of Ireland, who was landed there in 1807 (it is uncertain whether it was at his request, or against his will). He grew vegetables which he traded to whaling ships for rum. He has also been accused of kidnapping and enslaving visiting sailors. In 1809 he stole a whaleboat while the crew was obtaining water and left with five of his slaves. He arrived in Guayaquil alone. The island was also the home of the "Dog King", who was said to keep his people in order with a regiment of fierce canines. He fled after a rebellion of his "subjects." In about 1829 the government of Ecuador sent the first shipload of convicts to Floreana. Jose Villamil, a native of Louisiana, took some of the convicts and left for Chatham in 1832. The workers resented the harsh discipline and he fled for his life. When Darwin arrived in 1835, there were between two and three hundred in the penal colony. He described the settlement "placed about four and a half miles inland, and at a height probably of a thousand feet. . . .The homes are irregularly scattered over a flat space of ground, which is cultivated with sweet potatoes and bananas. The inhabitants although complaining of poverty, obtain, without much trouble, the means of subsistence. In the woods there are many wild pigs and goats; but the staple article of animal food is supplied by the tortoises." Darwin also found a party sent out from the Floreana colony on James, where they were engaged in salting tortoise meat and drying fish. By 1870 a Senor Valdizan was working with the colony of convicts collecting a lichen called Dyers Moss, used in fabric dyes. He was murdered and the remnants of the colony fought each other for a while before all left Floreana, some returning to mainland Ecuador, others joining the colony on San Cristobal. One of the curiosities remaining on Floreana is the post office barrel that was erected on the island sometime in the late 18th century by a passing ship. It is marked on a navigation chart as early as 1793. Ships, mainly from England would leave mail in this barrel in the hopes that it would be picked up by a ship passing in the opposite direction and conveyed back to Europe. It is said that information discovered here during the War of 1812 helped the American Navy virtually destroy the English whaling fleet. By the early 1900s someone had erected a roof over the barrel to keep it dry in rain and from being dried out by the sun. The tradition continues today. Mail placed in the box for all over the world, with no stamps, is left for others heading in that general direction to pick up and deliver. If you would like your mail postmarked stop first at Black Beach where Margret

The post office barrel on Floreana.

Wittmer, or her successor, will affix the barrel post office cancellation stamps. Near the post office box there are remnants of a fish factory founded by Norwegians in 1925. The colony was also to include fruitgrowing and canning. Some sources indicate there were as many as 22 Norwegians in the first group, but that the ship carrying a second contingent of settlers sank, and those left in the Galapagos were so disheartened they stayed less than five years. Fish tanks and steps leading to buildings that no longer exist are all that is left of the enterprise today. Some of the settlers moved to San Cristobal and others were the nucleus of a Scandinavian settlement on Santa

Cruz. Hard on the heels of the Norwegians in 1929 came a pair of German settlers, Dore Strauch Koerwin, and Friedrich Ritter, a self-styled philosopher who was fascinated with Robinson Crusoe stories. Before leaving Germany they had arranged for his wife to be housekeeper for Dore's husband. Friedrich and Dore built a home on Floreana they called Friedo (after themselves) in an extinct volcano crater five hundred feet above sea level to the east of the island's central mountain. In 1832 a small fishing boat landed another couple from Germany, Heinz and Margret Wittmer, with his young son, Harry, and two Alsatian dogs. Drawn by romantic magazine stories

Post office barrel cancellation stamps.
The top stamp also has the initials of the postmaster,
Margret Wittmer.

describing the life of Friedrich and Dore, they set up housekeeping in the abandoned pirate caves where their son Rolf was born on New Year's Day 1933, the first child born on Floreana, and perhaps in the entire archipelago. Prior to the baby's arrival a third group of settlers came in the fall of 1832. This group included an Austrian "baroness", two German men, Rudolf Lorenz and Robert Phillippson, and an Ecuadorian servant. It was the plan of the Baroness to build a hotel to attract rich Americans to the peace of the islands. In March of 1934 the Baroness and Philippson vanished, with no explanation despite an officially inquiry. In November Lorenz and a Norwegian fisherman were found dead on Marchena Island, apparent victims of a shipwreck, and Dr. Ritter, the vegetarian, died from eating spoiled chicken. Dore returned to Germany. Heinz died in 1963, but the rest of the Wittmers still live on Floreana, now at Black Beach (Puerto Velasco Ibarra), and Margret has served for years as the postmistress of the community, as well as of the post office letterbox. Her son Rolf is a tour boat captain, whose boat, the *Tip Top II*, is especially in demand because of its access to a source of fresh water, the family spring on Floreana. Guests aboard the boat are sometimes invited to the Wittmer home for dinner and to meet Margret and her daughter, Ingeborg Floreanita, born in 1937, and the second and third generation of Floreana-born Wittmers. Margret has written a book about the family's experiences in the Galapagos called *Floreana*. Originally published in German, it was later translated into English, and an Spanish edition is also available. A second, somewhat speculative book, that covers the unusual events on Floreana, is *The Galapagos Affair*, by John Treherne. In addition to the jetty at Black Beach, and the wet landing at Post Office Bay, Punta Cormorant on the northern shore is a favorite place for visitors to Floreana. Here there is a brown-colored sand beach with olivine crystals that give it a faintly greenish tinge. Just inland from the green beach is a flamingo lagoon, with other wading birds. Around the point from Punta Cormorant is a formation known as Devil's Crown, a half submerged crater which serves as a nesting ground for Red-billed Tropicbirds and offers excellent snorkeling. Floreana is the only island where the Medium Tree Finch lives. The Charles Mockingbird, originally endemic to the island, no longer resides there but may be found in limited numbers on Gardner-near-Charles and Champion, two smaller islands off the east coast of Floreana.

Fernandina

Fernandina is the westernmost island of the main group. It is named for Ferdinand of Aragon, the King of Spain who supported Columbus. The English name most commonly applied to the island was Narborough, for Admiral John Narborough. Geologically, it is one of the newest islands, and its most prolific vegetation is the lava cactus (Brachycereus nesioticus) which is usually the first plantlife to gain a foothold on cooled lava. Several kinds of lava are evident near the coast, and visitors should watch for fissures, some very narrow, some too large to leap across, that formed as the lava cooled. The crater on Fernandina has shown signs of life beginning in 1958 with a small eruption, and a decade later with the collapse of the crater floor accompanied by earthquakes. The main visitor site on the island is at Punta Espinoza on the northeast shore. It is a dry landing at most tide levels in an area of mangrove trees where the rare Mangrove Finch has occasionally been seen. The island features the largest colony of marine iguanas, draped over like-colored rocks. It is the nesting place for a small colony of Galapagos Penguins and until about 1988 the Flightless Cormorant was found here, but in subsequent years, although an occasional bird visits the shores of Fernandina, the cormorant has been decidedly harder to find. At high tide there are also some nice sandy pools near the shore, excellent for cavorting with sea lions. For the adventurous, longer hiking trips to the rim of the caldera may sometimes be arranged with the National Park Service.

Isabela

Isabela (named for Queen Isabela of Spain) is by a considerable margin, the largest island of the archipelago. Shaped roughly like a backwards letter "L" it is 81 miles long and 47 miles wide at its widest point, roughly 1771 square miles in area. The English name for Isabela is Albemarle, named for the Duke of Albemarle. The most striking physical feature of the island is five volcanos, called, north to south, Wolf, Darwin, Alcedo, Santo Tomas (also known as Sierra Negra) and Cerro Azul. The geological theory is that there is a "hot spot" that has created, in turn, each of Isabela's volcanoes. The hot spot remains stationary while the seafloor plate moves, leaving a trail of volcanic peaks. The last eruption on Isabela occurred in 1979 at Cerro Azul, but a fumarole in the caldera of Alcedo continues to be a valuable landmark for hikers. Isabela was a frequent stop for whaling ships beginning in the eighteenth century. Some historians have written that it was the fresh water available at some of the Galapagos Islands, and the availability of fresh meat in the form of the easily-caught, easily-stored tortoises that made the whaling and fur seal industries possible. In a few places there are remains of rock corrals used by the sailors as a holding area for tortoises. A familiar harbor for the whaling fleet was at Tagus Cove, a sheltered area facing Fernandina which still bears the carved signatures left by the crews of many visiting ships. In 1825 *H.M.S. Blonde* visited Tagus Cove on the way to Hawaii with the bodies of King Kamehameha II and his queen, who had died of measles on a visit to England. Darwin visited the island during his 1835 trip and hiked inland to a salt lake near the volcano which was later given his name. He concluded that at least the northern part of the island was "miserably sterile." In 1893 Don Antonio Gil of Guayaquil began the settlement of Puerto Villamil on the southern shore of

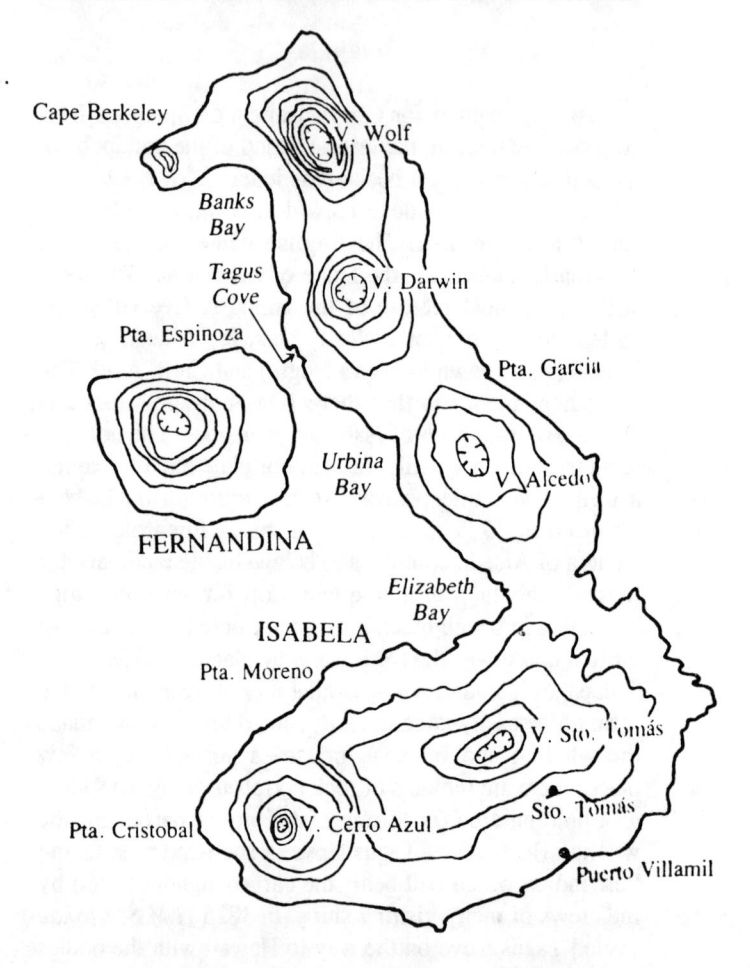

The volcanoes of Isabela are thought to have been created by the same geological "hot spot".

Isabela, and, later, Santo Tomas, about 2000 feet up the southern slope of the volcano by the same name, north of Villamil. By the turn of the century there were about 200 colonists in the upper colony who made a living digging sulphur from the crater wall and rounding up the wild cattle of the island to sell as fresh or dried meat to passing ships. During World War I a German fleet, commanded by Admiral Von Spee stopped at Villamil for fresh meat on its way to the Falkland Islands. Although the southern portion of Isabela is seldom visited by tourists, the settlement at Villamil is growing and includes at least four houses offering accommodations and meals. The first recorded aircraft to visit the Galapagos Islands came in 1934 to Isabela in response to a radio message that a naturalist named William Robinson had suffered an attack of appendicitis at Tagus Cove. The message had been relayed to the U. S. Navy at Panama, and seaplanes with a doctor aboard were sent to the cove. The operation was a success and the patient recovered. Isabela has a number of visitor sites, the most popular at Tagus Cove where there is a dry landing, and visitors can view (but may not add to) the historical graffiti on the cliffs and walk inland on a fairly strenuous uphill path to the salt lake and a view of the Darwin volcano. A visit to Tagus Cove frequently concludes with a panga ride along the base of the high cliffs to see the seabird nesting area. To the south, but still along the west coast, is Urbina Bay where there is a wet landing and a chance to view coral uplifted by earthquake activity in 1954. Still further south at the bend in the L is Elizabeth Bay where a panga ride along the cliffs offers views of penguins, large mangrove trees along the shoreline (and the best chance for Mangrove Finch), and turtle lagoons. From this point there are also several dramatic views of Sierra Negra volcano. At Punta Moreno on the north coast of the bottom section of Isabela, there is a dry landing and a trail over lava fields with several different types of lava. Here, too, are often found

Flightless Cormorants and occasionally Flamingos and other shorebirds in green lagoons that occur, oasis-like, on the otherwise sterile lava. There is a dry landing on the south coast at Puerto Villamil although it is largely unprotected and can be difficult in a rough sea or at some tide levels. This area is considered the best water and shorebird area in the archipelago, containing both salt and brackish lagoons, plus rocky, muddy and sandy shoreline, and coastal waters. It is possible to visit the highlands from Puerto Villamil, up to the rim of the Sierra Negra volcano. On the eastern side of Isabela Flightless Cormorants may usually be viewed from a panga near Punta Garcia, opposite the island of James. To the south is a wet landing beach that is the starting place for a trek to Alcedo volcano, known for its population of giant tortoises. It is a long hike (at least two days) and arrangements can be made to camp at several designated areas on the slopes of the volcano and on its rim. Application for a camping permit must be made to the National Park office at Academy Bay. It is against park rules to build a campfire, but gasoline or kerosene stoves are permitted.

Roca Redonda

About 30 kilometers north of the northern tip of Isabella is Roca Redonda (Round Rock). Called "the aviary of the ocean" by Herman Melville, it is the nesting place of several seabird colonies including the Wedge-rumped Storm Petrel. The rock, which rises abruptly from the water is only a few acres at the top, but is said by geologists to be the tip of a huge underwater mountain 12 miles across at the base. Unless there is considerable haze the rock can be viewed as you round Cape Berkeley at the north west tip of Isabela.

James

James was named for King James II of England and is often called Santiago, Spanish for James, although its official Spanish name is San Salvador (the first landfall of Columbus in the new world). It is located east of Isabela and northwest of Santa Cruz. James was an early stopping place for pirates and whaling ships, the first recorded visitor being the ships Bachelor's Delight and Nicholas in 1684. Here they could find salt, lots of tortoises, firewood, and fresh water during the rainy season. Pirates really did stop at Buccaneer Bay, and some South American pottery shards found near there are said to be from a stolen shipment of quince jam. In 1813 the U. S. Frigate *Essex* rested off the shore of James Island taking a pause from its mission, the destruction of the British whaling fleet, during the War of 1812. One of the ship's officers, John Cowan, went ashore to settle a dispute with a fellow officer, Lieutenant Gamble of the marines, by dueling. Cowan was killed and buried with full military honors on the beach. The captain left a bottle with a message for another officer at the head of the grave. The bottle and message did not reach the man intended and have never been found. When Darwin visited James Island in 1835, he tells of visiting a spot near a salt lake where "a few years since the sailors belonging to a sealing-vessel murdered their captain in this quiet spot; and we saw his skull lying among the bushes." The two tales may be two separate homicides, or they may be the same incident, muddled by time. During his visit Darwin also found a party of Spaniards from the colony on Floreana who had been sent to dry fish and salt tortoise meat. About six miles inland, at a height of 2000 feet, two men whose job it was to catch the tortoises lived in a small shelter. Darwin spent one night here. He also accompanied some of the Spaniards to the salt lake where water only three or four inches deep rested on a layer of beautifully crystallized white salt. It was this reservoir of salt that gave impetus to the last commercial venture on James. After World War II a company brought equipment and nearly a hundred workers to the island bent on extracting the salt. The project was given up about 1971, but two families, and, later, a single caretaker were employed until 1984 to guard the equipment and keep the company's mineral rights active. A small house still stands on the coastal bluff of James, along with assorted rusting machinery and the skeleton of a warehouse. The main effect that the history of habitation has had on the island is the presence of a large and prolific goat population (said to be over 100,000), some wild burros, and a number of feral pigs. The pigs and goats are being attacked as part of a non-indigenous animal extermination program. Many boats have goat stew for dinner after a visit to James. Land iguanas are extinct on the island due to the depredation of goats and pigs. The commonest site for visitors is at Puerto Egas in James Bay on the west coast of the island. It is a wet landing on the black sands. Trails lead inland to the spring, and to the salt mine crater and the remains of the mining operation. Another trail leads around the coastal area to the fur seal grotto where both sea lions and Galapagos Fur Seals sleep on the black rocks and sand and swim in a series of rocky pools. Espumilla Beach is north of Puerto Egas and separated from it by lava fields which are difficult to cross. A wet landing on these black sands gives the visitor access to a pair of lagoons often populated by flamingos, ducks, and other shore birds, and a turtle nesting beach. Buccaneer Cove, where pirates often anchored, can be visited by boat, but there are no good landing places. On the northeast shore of James is Sullivan Bay where a dry landing is possible in a calm sea. The area is interesting for its array of lava left from eruptions early in this century and still uneroded.

Bartolome

Bartolome, in English, Bartholemew, named for Lt. David Bartholemew of the British Royal Navy, is a small island just off the east coast of James. Located just a little over 20 miles from Santa Cruz and Baltra it is a popular place for day trips. There is a dry landing on the northwest coast of Bartolome which is the start of a half-hour walk to the summit of an extinct volcano. The view from the top, looking back toward Pinnacle Rock (a triangular rock jutting out of the water at the edge of the bay below) is one of the most photographed in the entire archipelago. From the slopes of the volcano, visitors can also see a number of interesting lava formations including solidified volcanic "bubbles" in the water and a series of spatter cones on land to the east. A wet landing on the white shell-sand beach southwest of the large cone brings visitors to a narrow neck of land with a white sand beach on either side, connected with a about a half mile trail through the mangroves. The south beach is a turtle nesting area. Off the north beach the water is deeper, and penguins are often included among your swimming companions.

Jervis

Jervis, named for Admiral John Jervis, in Spanish is known as Rabida, for the convent "de la Rabida." Its most striking feature is a deep red sand beach well populated by sea lions of all sizes. Just beyond the beach is a lagoon where some of the bachelor sea lions hang out, along with the usual lagoon avifauna, flamingos, ducks, and shorebirds. The brushy area around the lagoon is also a good place to look for finches.

Tower

Tower was apparently named for its towering cliffs. Its Spanish name is Genovesa, to honor Genoa, Italy, the traditional birthplace of Columbus. It is the northernmost island usually visited by tourists, an eight-hour journey in the fastest tour boat from Santa Cruz. The main attraction on Tower is the Red-footed Booby, a bird seldom seen on any of the other islands. On Tower it is hard to miss. When you anchor in Darwin Bay, it is usually only a short time until the railing on the bow of your boat is lined with soft brown immature Red-footed Boobies that will turn their heads to follow a gesturing hand like a row of marionettes. There are two visitor sites within the curved shelter of the bay on Tower's southern coast. The Darwin Bay trail starts with a wet landing on a white sand beach and continues to the west on gently sloping terrain. Nesting birds include the Red-footed Booby, the Masked Booby, and the Great Frigatebird. It is also an excellent place for a number of other birds that can be seen on other islands, but seem to be easier to find on Tower including the Galapagos Dove, the Yellow-crowned Night Heron, the Galapagos Mockingbird, and no less than four finches: the Large Ground Finch, the Sharp-beaked Ground Finch, the Large Cactus Finch and the Warbler Finch. The white sand beach is excellent swimming although Darwin Bay has only a small sea lion population. The second visitor site on Darwin Bay begins with a dry landing at Prince Phillip's Steps, a natural stone stairway up the cliff that looks more difficult to navigate than it is, but does require careful stepping. On the top of the cliff a trail leads through many nesting birds (including both Great and Magnificient Frigatebirds) to the seaward side of the peninsula where a colony of more than 200,000 pair of Wedge-rumped Storm Petrels blackens the sky from April to late September, although a few birds are nearly always present. Band-rumped Storm Petrels also nest on Tower, but they are entirely nocturnal and rarely seen by visitors. Also present on the rocky cliffs are large numbers of Audubon's Shearwaters, Swallow-tailed Gulls, and a few Red-billed Tropicbirds. This is also one of the best places in the archipelago for some of the oceanic accidentals like Franklin Gull and Fairy Tern.

Smaller Islands

In addition to the islands already listed there are some smaller islands often visited by tourists including Chinaman's Hat (named for its shape) near James, and Daphne, between James and Baltra, where the Galapagos Martin may be found. The triangle formed by Isabela on the west, James on the north, and Santa Cruz on the east is the location of many small islands including Duncan (Pinzon), Guy Fawkes, Beagle, and Nameless (Sin Nombre). Dotted about the eastern coast of Floreana are Champion, Enderby, Caldwell, Gardner-near-Floreana, and Watson. About the same latitude but east of Tower Island are Marchena (Bindloe) and Abingdon (Pinta), and way up to the northwest are Wolf (Wenman) and Darwin (Culpepper). In addition there are countless small islets and rock outcroppings.

Miscellaneous

MONEY: The currency of Ecuador is based on the sucre, usually written S/, named for General Sucre who defeated the Spanish in 1824 paving the way for Ecuadorian independence. There are bills of 5, 10, 20, 50, 100, 500 and 1000 sucres, and a one sucre coin. There used to be smaller denomination coins called centavos, but they are little used now. It is difficult to change money in the islands and even harder to change travelers checks. A few places in Puerto Ayora will accept credit cards although they would rather not. Except for shopping and perhaps a meal off of the boat at Academy Bay, there is little need for cash. Most tourist boats will let you run up a bar tab (and a tab at the snack bar and boutique if your ship has one), and will permit you to settle up for traveler's checks, cash, or even American money at the end of the voyage.

DRESS: Dress is very informal on a Galapagos Islands trip. The smaller boats tend to be less formal than the larger vessels. The weather is usually warm enough for shorts and short-sleeved shirts, although a sweater or long-sleeved jacket is occasionally needed in the evening. The volcanic rock is rough and can be very hot from the sun, so a pair of athletic or other good walking shoes and socks

From the top of Bartolome looking toward Pinnacle Rock.

is needed ashore. Many prefer true hiking boots. Most boats, especially the smaller ones, do not require or encourage the wearing of shoes on board. On one boat the crew seldom donned footwear except when entering the engine room. A bathing suit, two if possible, is important equipment for a Galapagos trip. Most boats have some space that is suitable for the drying of wet suits and a limited amount of hand-washed laundry. Many women bring a caftan or other loose-fitting informal garment to wear to the late dinner after they have cleaned up from a day ashore.

ELECTRICITY: Power on the Eduadorian mainland is 110 volts, 60 cycles. Power available on cruise ships can vary. Many boats have two separate power systems. A 110 volt system for use when the engines are running and a battery operated system for use at anchor.

SUN: The Galapagos islands sit right on the equator, and the sun can be intense. Because the air, cooled by the water, is often not especially hot it is easy to get a severe sunburn before you notice it. Sun screen is imperative for most people, and a wide-brimmed hat is a good idea. There are excellent buys on Panama-style woven hats in the Indian markets on the mainland.

ON THE SEA: The Galapagos Islands are in the Pacific Ocean, and there are many times that the boat is out of sight of land. Especially on the smaller boats the wave motion can be quite noticeable and seasickness can strike even those who sail frequently back home so it is best to be prepared. Some respond well to Dramamine and similar medicine. Many have had excellent success with adhesive patches containing Scopolomine that are placed behind the ear and dispense medication over a three-day period. These patches require a prescription from your physician and are not available on the islands. If you become ill after applying the patch or if there is a change in behavior (hallucinations are one of the side effects that occasionally occur), discontinue use immediately.

AQUATIC MAMMALS: The waters around the Galapagos host many different kinds of whales and dolphins. Whales are unpredictable; depending on the season, the current, and the temperature of the water, likely species include the finback, minke, humpback, sei, pilot, orca (or killer) and occasionally a large sperm whale. Both the white-bellied and bottle-nosed dolphin are quite common. The bottle-nosed species is the one usually seen riding the bow wave of boats. As they swim close to the boat you can often hear their high pitched calls. On dark nights they seem to glow, outlined by the bioluminescence of thousands of tiny creatures which inhabit the top layers of the water and produce light when disturbed.

SWIMMING: Fun in the water with the animals is an exciting part of a Galapagos cruise. Even those reluctant to actually swim should bring a bathing suit so they can go wading with the sea lions. Swimming shoes are also useful for areas where marine creatures or rough rocks and shells might injure unprotected feet. An old pair of tennis shoes works fine. A mask and snorkel add a good deal of pleasure by giving visitors a window on the underwater world. To have a penguin dive suddenly right beside you, to see the marine iguana feeding on seaweed, and to watch the sea lions dive and romp is part of the Galapagos experience.

WATER: Freshwater is a precious commodity on the Galapagos Islands. To ensure sufficient and clean drinking water some tour companies, Nuevo Mundo for example, give each of their clients a gallon of water to take aboard the plane as carry-on luggage. Some boats have basins but no showers or furnish only a saltwater shower on deck. Nearly all boat captains, by sign or lecture, urge passengers to use as little water as possible. On one boat that had private facilities, the guide informed the guests that each was entitled to two minutes of water per day. Either one two-minute shower, two one-minute showers, or four 30-second bursts. There was no way to monitor compliance, but once the problem is understood most visitors are cooperative. Unless assured that it is safe, don't drink the water from shipboard water taps. If bottled water is available, it is probably best not to drink tap water even if it has been treated. Shipboard toilets use a saltwater flush and many have unusual flushing mechanisms. On the first day a crew member, or the guide, will demonstrate the procedure. If you have any questions, or experience any problems, call for help immediately.

FOOD: Most of the meals are served aboard your touring boat. In general, you get what you pay for. As one guidebook observed, "The cheaper the boat, the more rice and fish you can expect to eat." That remark is not meant to downgrade Ecuadorean rice and fish, for it can be excellent. Often while you are touring an island the boat's crew (including the captain) is catching fish for lunch or dinner. Every dinner (the main meal of the day, whether served at noon or night) is begun with soup, sometimes a meat or fish broth base, and sometimes made from vegetable broth. Fresh fruits and vegetables are the backbone of Ecuadorian cooking, and fruit juices the most common drink. In South America they have many fruits that are unknown to the average North American. In addition to the vegetable tomato, they have a tomato that is a fruit, sometimes called a tree tomato. Tomato ice cream is a favorite confection. They also have Chirimoya with a custardlike inside, Mamey with red sweet squash-like meat, Pepinos (sweet white and purple striped, like a cucumber) and many varieties of melon. Sometimes as many as five different kinds of fruit will be served for breakfast. Bananas are another food staple. Fried bananas are a frequent side dish with lunch, and banana pancakes an especially tasty breakfast.

LANGUAGE: The language of the Galapagos is Spanish. When choosing a tour boat, if you are not making the plans through a North American tour agency, be sure to specify that you want a guide who speaks English. All guides are trained and certified through the Darwin

Research Station and are very knowledgeable in the natural history of the islands, and most English-speaking guides speak fairly good English, some excellent. There are also many who speak German, and a few conversant in French, Norwegian, and other languages. The captain and members of the ship's crew often do not speak English, or, if they do, their vocabulary is limited to the subjects and words needed to do their job. Storekeepers and others ashore often know little English. If you took Spanish in high school or college, brush up on it before you go. Not only will it make business transactions easier, but it might win you new friends.

TIPPING: At the end of the voyage a tip is expected. On most boats the tip is given to the captain and shared with the crew. The guide is usually tipped separately. The average tip is $1.50 to $2 a day per person.

BOOKS: The Galapagos Islands have caught the imagination of travelers and writers since they were first discovered. In preparation for a trip it is a good idea to read some of the old accounts, or better yet, take a couple of them along with you for shipboard reading. Must reading includes the chapter on the Galapagos archipelago in Charles Darwin's *The Voyage of the Beagle*, and *The Encantadas or Enchanted Isles*, by Herman Melville. If the subject interests you it might be good to give at least a brief reading to Darwin's *On the Origin of Species*, which was written long after his voyage, but is an outgrowth of research on the Galapagos. There are also biographies of Darwin available, one of the best is Irving Stone's *The Origin*, also *Darwin and the Beagle*, by Alan Moorhead (1969, Harper), which concentrates on the Galapagos trip. *Galapagos—World's End*, by writer-naturalist William Beebe, originally published in the 1920s, was reprinted in 1988 by Dover. There are at least three books covering the birds, beasts, geology, and plants of the island (perhaps more than you want to know). They are *Galapagos; A Natural History Guide*, by M. H. Jackson (1985, University of Calgary Press), *Darwin's Islands; A Natural History of the Galapagos*, by Ian Thornton (1971, American Museum of Natural History), and *Galapagos— Noah's Ark of the Pacific*, by I. Eibl-Eibesfeldt (1961, Doubleday). The standard birding guide is *A Field Guide to the Birds of the Galapagos*, by Michael Harris (1974, revised 1983, Collins). For lighter reading, and just for fun, try Kurt Vonnegut's science fiction novel Galapagos. If you take it with you it will add an eerie dimension to your trip. There are also a number of annually published travel guides to Ecuador, or South America, that include a section on the Galapagos. The National Park has a small guide booklet available. Tui de Roi Moore, a noted Galapago photographer, has a beautiful picture book *Islands Lost in Time*.

DEPARTURE: There is a departure tax of $20 U. S. on international flights. This amount may be paid in sucres. Be sure to arrive at the airport in plenty of time as outward bound customs and ticketing is often very slow. More than two hours is recommended. The national airlines, Ecuatoriana, sometimes does not serve breakfast, even on early morning flights. Grab what you can at the airport, or stock up the night before.

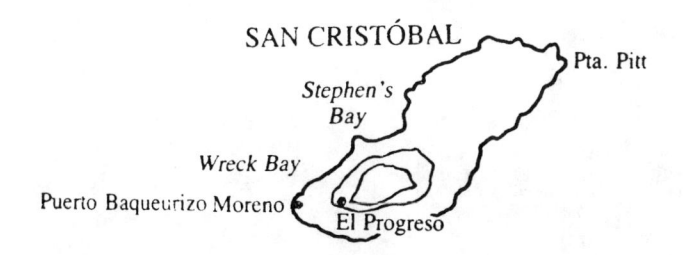

SAN CRISTÓBAL
Pta. Pitt
Stephen's Bay
Wreck Bay
Puerto Baquerizo Moreno
El Progreso

The Enchanted Isles of Ecuador are far from the beaten path for most travelers. In visiting them you are close to nature and subject to the dictates of the sea. Thus, when you make your visit, some specific piece of information we offer here may no longer be totally correct. Please remember that travel requires flexibility and adaptability. A good traveler is willing to experience a new and different place with an appreciation of nature's diversity.

We have traveled for more than 20 years, have visited over 30 nations, and have never been truly glad to leave any country. The North American traveler has a reputation, somewhat undeserved, of insisting on the best facilities, and then looking at the history and culture around him and finding them lacking in comparison to the brilliance of his own nation. We know you're not like that.

This book offers an opportunity to learn in advance about some of the little things that might be stumbling blocks in your travels. We hope that this enhances your trip. A confident and enthusiastic traveler is one of the best ambassadors a country can send forth.

Happy traveling.

Kit and Art Lane

Coming Soon—
New *Traveler's Previews*
Planned for 1990:

RUSSIA

WINTER IN SPAIN

AFRICAN SAFARI

A TRAVELER'S PREVIEW

by Kit and Art Lane

FIJI

For many people Fiji is a place in the imagination, more remote than Tahiti, but not as wild as Borneo. Present-day Fiji offers the traveler a chance to experience the South Pacific in a country where nearly everyone speaks some English. This *Traveler's Preview* will help you find the smaller roads and singular attractions, and cope with everyday differences. What does a Fijian mean when he says, "Bula"? Why do you take off your sunglasses when you meet a chief?

AUSTRALIA

Australia, the land down under, is the opposite of North America in many ways. The steaming rain forests are in the north, the more temperate climate in the south. They have picnics on the beach at Christmas time, and ski in August. Most Australian birds, mammals and marsupials are found nowhere else in the world. Yet it is a comfortable trip for most North Americans. The language is mostly familiar, they can read the signs, and sometimes have pizza for dinner. But to fully experience the country this *Traveler's Preview* will guide you through ordering from a ten-page dinner menu, riding the excellent public transportation systems, and coping with the peculiarities of Australian electrical cords.

Each volume, $5.95 at your local book store or travel supply store.

Or send name, address, and check (plus $1 for shipping) to:

> PAVILION PRESS
> P.O. Box 250
> Douglas, MI 49406